1 MONTH OF
FREE
READING

at

www.ForgottenBooks.com

By purchasing this book you are eligible for one month membership to ForgottenBooks.com, giving you unlimited access to our entire collection of over 1,000,000 titles via our web site and mobile apps.

To claim your free month visit:

www.forgottenbooks.com/free1121166

ISBN 978-0-331-41878-1
PIBN 11121166

Town of Fremont

ANNUAL REPORTS

OF THE

Selectmen, Treasurer

AND ALL OTHER

Officers and Committees

FOR THE

Financial Year Ending January 31, 1938

THE CLARKE PRESS
MANCHESTER, N. H.
1938

TOWN OFFICERS

Clerk
WILLIAM T. SHANNON

Selectmen
GEORGE A. BASSETT, 1938
ALBERT G. FULLER, 1939
E. ABBOTT BEEDE, 1910

Treasurer
GEORGE E. BEEDE

Collector
LAURENCE A. PETTENGILL

Auditor
NORMAN S. McINTOSH

Highway Agent
SYLVESTER A. SANBORN

Chief Fire Department
ROBERT W. SMITH

Health Officer
FRANK N. DAVIS

Librarian
BLANCHE M. MARCOTTE

Library Trustees
LULA M. BALL, 1938
BERTHA H. STEVENSON, 1939
GEORGE A. BASSETT, 1940

Trustees of Trust Funds
EUGENE D. SANBORN, 1938
HENRY A. COOK, 1939
ALBERT G. FULLER, 1940

Dog Officer
MOSES A. SEAVEY

Constable
ROBERT W. SMITH

Police
ROBERT W. SMITH, CHIEF

LEE B. MOULTON

Forest Fire Warden
ROBERT W. SMITH

Deputy Forest Fire Wardens
ALBERT G. FULLER   LEE B. MOULTON
CURTICE S. SANBORN   SYLVESTER A. SANBORN

Moderator
EUGENE D. SANBORN

Supervisors of the Check List
ARTHUR A. DAVIES

CURTICE S. SANBORN

SYLVESTER A. SANBORN

Ballot Inspectors
GLADYS B. AHEARN   JOSEPH P. BASSETT
ANDREW J. BROWN   SARAH L. CLEMENT

Janitor of Town Hall
LEE B. MOULTON

Budget Committee
WILLIAM COLE

JOHN H. ELLIS

EUGENE D. SANBORN, members at large.
George A. Bassett, member from Board of Selectmen.
Norman S. McIntosh, member from School Board.

Representative to the General Court
CLIFTON H. BEEDE

TOWN WARRANT

To the Inhabitants of the Town of Fremont in the County of Rockingham, in said State, qualified to vote in Town Affairs:

[L. S.]

You are hereby notified to meet at the Town Hall in said Fremont on Tuesday, the eighth day of March, next, at ten of the clock in the forenoon, to act upon the following subjects:

1. To choose all necessary Town Officers for the year ensuing.

2. To bring in your vote for a delegate to the State Constitutional Convention.

3. To hear the report of the Budget Committee and act thereon.

4. To raise and appropriate such sums of money as may be deemed necessary for the following purposes: care of cemeteries, street lighting, support of poor, maintenance of highways and bridges, general expenses of highway department, the Public Library, observance of Memorial Day, and for town charges.

5. To see whether the town will vote to accept class II or Class V aid from the State on highways and raise and appropriate either $1,500.00 for Class II or $243.90 for Class V highway construction.

6. On petition of Clifton H. Beede and twenty-six others: To see of the Town will vote to raise and appropriate the sum of $1,500.00 for the permanent improvement of the Sandown road (so called) leading from route 109 Fremont Village to Sandown town line, said sum of money to be expended in conjunction with any appropriation that may be made by the State for said purpose, under the direction of the State Highway Commissioner.

7.   To see if the town will vote to permit the use of rifles in hunting deer.

8.   To see if the town will vote to authorize the Selectmen to borrow money in anticipation of taxes.

9.   To see what action the town will take in regard to Real Estate taken for non-payment of taxes.

10.   To sec if the town will vote to raise and appropriate a sum of money to meet Federal requirements for W. P. A. projects.

11.   To transact any other business that may legally come before the meeting.

Given under our hands and seal, this 21st day of February, in the year of our Lord nineteen hundred and thirty-eight.

> GEORGE A. BASSETT,
> ALBERT G. FULLER,
> E. ABBOTT BEEDE,
> *Selectmen of Fremont*

A true copy of Warrant—Attest:

> GEORGE A. BASSETT,
> ALBERT G. FULLER,
> E. ABBOTT BEEDE,
> *Selectmen of Fremont*

BUDGET OF THE TOWN OF

Estimates of Revenue and Expenditures for the Ensuing

Actual Revenue and Expenditures of the Previous

Sources of Revenue	Actual revenue previous year, 1937	Estimated revenue ensuing year, 1938	In-crease	De-crease
FROM STATE:				
Interest and Dividends Tax	$105.82	$105.82	....	....
Insurance Tax	14.69	14.69	....	....
Railroad Tax	29.62	29.62	....	....
Savings Bank Tax	609.82	609.82	....	....
For Fighting Forest Fires	1.84	1.84	....	....
Relief Apportionment	184.49	84.49	....	100.00
FROM LOCAL SOURCES EXCEPT TAXES:				
Business Licenses and Permits and Fees	12.00	12.00	....	....
Rent of Town Hall and Other Buildings	274.00	274.00	....	....
Interest Received on Taxes and Deposits	33.88	33.88	....	....
Income of Departments:				
(a) Highway, including rental of equipment	63.00	63.00	....	....
(b) Cement	4.20	....	....	4.20
(c) Cemetery Lots Sold	20.00	....	....	20.00
(d) Wire	2.00	....	....	2.00
(e) Town Maps	7.00	....	....	7.00
Fire Co. Hose	14100	....	....	141.00
(f) Balance in full on True Barn	25.00	....	....	25.00
Motor Vehicle Permit Fees	609.18	609.18	....	....
FROM LOCAL TAXES OTHER THAN PROPERTY TAXES:				
(a) Poll Taxes	718.00	675.00	....	43.00
Dog Licenses	144.25	144.25	....	....
TOTAL REVENUES FROM ALL SOURCES EXCEPT PROPERTY TAXES	2,999.79	2,657.59	....	342.20
AMOUNT TO BE RAISED BY PROPERTY TAXES	16,350.63	15,097.46	....	....
TOTAL REVENUES	$19,350.42	$17,755.05	....	....

Year, February 1, 1938, to January 31, 1939, Compared With

Year, February 1, 1937, to January 31, 1938

PURPOSES OF EXPENDITURES	Actual expenditures previous year, 1937	Estimated expenditures ensuing year, 1938	Increase	Decrease
CURRENT MAINTENANCE				
Expenses:				
General Government:				
Town Officers' Salaries	$477.40	$477.40	....	....
Town Officers' Expenses	352.22	352.22	....	....
Election and Registration Expenses	75.00	110.00	35.00	....
Expenses Town Hall and Other Town Buildings	672.20	322.20	....	350.00
Protection of Persons and Property:				
Police Department	49.31	50.00	.69	....
Fire Department	1,232.21	176.00	....	1,056.21
Moth Extermination—Blister Rust, Forest Fires	3.68	53.68	50.00	....
Health:				
Health Department, including hospitals	16.46	56.46	40.00	....
Vital Statistics	5.10	5.10	....	....
Highways and Bridges:				
Town maintenance	1,794.19	1,500.00	....	294.19
Street Lighting	300.00	300.00	....	....
General Expenses of Highway Department—$749.08 less Truck Plow, 270.00	479.08	750.00	270.92	....
W.P.A. Project	....	1,000.00	1,000.00	....
Libraries:				
Libraries	86.91	75.00	....	11.91
Public Welfare:				
Town Poor	946.24	400.00	....	546.24
Old Age Assistance	268.80	300.00	31.20	....
Patriotic Purposes:				
Memorial Day and Other Celebrations	160.00	150.00	....	10.00
Public Service Enterprises:				
Cemeteries	72.80	170.00	97.20	....
OUTLAY FOR NEW CONSTRUCTION AND PERM. IMPROVE.				
Highways and Bridges:				
State Aid Construction—Town's Share, S. A. Y.	1,490.40	1,500.00	9.60	....
New Equipment—Blade Plow	270.00	....	....	270.00
PAYMENTS TO OTHER GOVERN-MENTAL DIVISIONS:				
State Taxes	1,632.00	1,224.00	....	408.00
County Taxes	2,282.99	2,782.99	500.00	....
Payments to Precincts	4,500.00	....	....	....
Payment to School Districts—1936—1937	3,602.00	....	....	....
Balance Due on Dog Tax	150.65	6,000.00	....	2.252.65
TOTAL EXPENDITURES	$20,919.64	$17,755.05	$2,034.61	$5,199.20

SELECTMEN'S REPORT

Inventory as made by the Selectmen April 1, 1937:

Real estate, resident	$296,490.00
Real estate, non-resident	81,885.00
Electric plants	8,956.00
Horses, 30	2,165.00
Cows, 119	7,000.00
Neat stock, 8	315.00
Fowl, 15,475	10,160.00
Wood & Lumber	· 1,200.00
Gasoline pumps & tanks	1,575.00
Stock in Trade	47,575.00
Mills & Machinery	87,700.00
	$545,021.00
Resident property tax	$13,376.55
Non-resident property tax	2,974.08
347 poll taxes, at $2.00	694.00
	$17,044.63

Rate of taxation on $1,000.00, $30.00
Exempted to soldiers $5,725.00

APPROPRIATIONS FOR 1937

State Tax	$1,632.00
County tax	2,282.99
Town charges	1,600.00
Maintenance of Highways	1,800.00
General expenses of Highways	1,000.00
Town Poor	1,000.00
Fire House	700.00
Fire Hose	300.00
Street Lighting	300.00
Truck Snow Plow	270.00
Legislative Special S. A. Y.	1,500.00
Cemeteries, care of	65.00
Memorial Day Observance	160.00
Library	75.00
Schools, support of	6,000.00
Overlay	213.64
	$18,898.63

SCHEDULE OF TOWN PROPERTY

Town Hall and land	$8,000.00
Furniture within above building	250.00
Library building	600.00
Furniture and books in above building	650.00
Police Department, equipment	10.00
Fire Department, land & buildings	2,500.00
Fire Department, equipment	2,500.00
Highway Department, equipment	3,000.00
Schoolhouses (4) and land	4,000.00
School equipment	500.00
Brentwood Mining & Chemical Co., land	100.00
George A. Dill, land	100.00
Joseph B. Proulx, land	50.00
	$22,260.00

TOWN CLERK'S REPORT

(From February 1, 1937 to March 9, 1937)

Received Town Officers' filing fees $7.00

Received for Automobile permits to the
    number of 37 ....   115.93

. Total amount paid town treasurer $122.93

HENRY A. COOK,
Town Clerk.

(From March 10, 1937 to January 31, 1938)

Received from Dog licenses issued:-

3 Male Dogs	@	1.00	$3.00
53 Male Dogs & spayed female dogs	@	2.00	106.00
9 Female Dogs	@	5.00	45.00

65     $154.00

Reserved for fees 65 @ 15 c 9.75

Paid to town treasurer $144.25

Licensed pool tables as follows:

To Victor B. Marcotte one table, July 1, 1937
    to December 31, 1937 .... $5.00

Paid to Town Treasurer $5.00

Received from permits issued for registration
of motor vehicles to the number of 176...... $493.25

Total amount paid town treasurer.......... $493.25

WILLIAM T. SHANNON,
Town Clerk

TAX COLLECTOR'S REPORT

Amount of Collector's Warrant $16,350.63
Polls, 348 at $2.00 .... 696.00
Subsequent Polls added, 4 at $2.00 .... 8.00
Interest & charges on poll taxes 1936 levy 3.42
Interest received on property taxes 1935-36-37 .. 30.46
Taxes 1936 .... 26.86
Tax sale 1935, redeemed 37.80
Uncollected poll taxes of 1936 collection 36.00

$17,189.17

Paid over to the Town Treasurer $17,181.17
Uncollected poll taxes of 1937 collection 8.00

LAWRENCE A. PETTENGILL,
Collector

TREASURER'S REPORT

Cash on hand February 1, 1937.............. $5,368.27

Received from all sources 20,412.37

    $25,780.64

Payments made on Selectmen's orders........ $22,215.25

Cash on hand January 31, 1938 .... $3,565.39

LIABILITIES

Due School District balance of 1937 appropriation $1,500.00

Due School District 1937 dog license money..   132.25

    $1,632.25

ASSETS

Cash on hand January 31, 1938 .... $3,565.39

Taxes bought and paid by town 245.19

Poll taxes due the town 8.00

    $3,818.58

Less total liabilities $1,632.25

Net amount of assets $2,186.33

GEORGE E. BEEDE.

Treasurer

SUMMARY OF RECEIPTS

From Local Taxes:
Property taxes, 1937 .... $16,350.63
Poll taxes, 1937 .... 696.00
Property taxes, previous years 64.62
Poll taxes, previous years 36.00
Interest and charges on taxes 33.88
From State:
State aid on relief expenditures 184.49
Interest and dividend tax 105.82
Insurance tax 14.69
Railroad tax 29.62
Savings bank tax 609.82
Forest fires 1.84
From Local Sources Except Taxes:
Rent of town hall 274.00
Dog licenses 144.25
Candidates filing fees 7.00
Pool table license 5.00
Registration of motor vehicles, 1937........ 568.75
Registration of motor vehicles, 1938........ 40.43
Town of Danville, plowing snow 63.00
Lyman S. Hooke, balance on fire hose 141.00
J. P. Bassett, cement 4.20
A. G. Fuller, roll of wire 2.00
A. G. Fuller, Gibson barn 25.00
Town maps (2) 7.00
Merton Healey, cemetery lot 20.00
Town note from Derry bank 983.33

Total Receipts $20,412.37

SUMMARY OF PAYMENTS

General Government:

Town officers' salaries	$477.40
Town officers' expenses	352.22
Election and registration expenses	75.00
Town Hall expenses	672.20

Protection of Persons and Property:

Police department	49.31
Fire department	235.89

Health:

Special quarantine for paralysis	16.46
Vital statistics	5.10

Highways and Bridges:

Town maintenance	1,794.19
Street lighting ..,...................	300.00
General expense of Highway department...	479.08

Libraries	86.91

Charities:

Old age assistance	268.80
Town poor	946.24

Memorial Day observance	160.00

Cemeteries	72.80

Unclassified:

Refund automobile tax, Mrs. Jennie West ...	4.25
Taxes bought by town	245.19
Discounts and abatements	49.50

New Construction and Improvements:

Special State Aid construction	1,490.40
Fire house and hose	1,000.00
New equipment; truck snow plow	270.00

Indebtedness:

Payment on note from Derry bank	996.67

Payment to other Governmental divisions:

Schools, balance of 1936 appropriation	3,752.65
Taxes paid to State	1,632.00
Taxes paid to County	2,282.99
Schools, 1937 appropriation	4,500.00
Total of all payments	$22,215.25

DETAILED STATEMENT OF PAYMENTS

GENERAL GOVERNMENT

Town Officers' Salaries:

George A. Bassett, Selectman	$100.40
Albert G. Fuller, Selectman	68.00
E. Abbott Beede, Selectman	74.00
Lawrence A. Pettengill, Collector	100.00
Blanche M. Marcotte, Librarian	52.00
George E. Beede, Treasurer	30.00
Henry A. Cook, Clerk	2.00
William T. Shannon, Clerk	25.00
Eugene D. Sanborn, Moderator	5.00
Moses A. Seavey, Dog Officer	10.00
Norman S. McIntosh, Auditor	6.00
Robert W. Smith, Constable	5.00
	$477.40

Town Officers' Expenses:

Asso. of N. H. Assessors, dues by law	$2.00
The Clarke Press, printing annual reports...	106.56
E. D. Sanborn, bonding town officers	50.00
Alfred B. Sargent, printing and stationery..	3.40
John W. A. Green, copying transfers	7.20
Joseph P. Melzer, supplies	2.10
Moses A. Seavey, dog officer's expense.....	2.00
W. P. Garrison, Publisher, auto guide......	3.75
Elmer D. Brown, surveyor	6.00
Ruth G. Fuller, copying records	5.00

William T. Shannon, Clerk:

Issuing 176 auto permits	44.00
Postage and stationery	2.60

Henry A. Cook, Clerk:
Issuing 37 auto permits	9.25
Postage	.16
Robert W. Smith, police badge	3.00
M. A. Willey, postage	6.98
Wheeler & Clark, supplies and printing	46.28

Lawrence A. Pettengill, Collector:
Sargent Bros., printing tax bills	5.25
Postage	4.86
Attending Tax Collector's meeting	5.00

George A. Bassett, Selectman:
Goodman's Book Store, supplies	2.80
Expenses attending Assessors' meeting	2.75
Expenses meeting with W.P.A. engineer, Portsmouth	3.65
Telephone, business calls	1.40
Use of car on town business, 64 miles at 5c	3.20
Dinner in Portsmouth	.60
Postage	.45

Albert G. Fuller, Selectman:
Use of car, 103 miles at 5c	5.15
Postage	.93
Telephone	2.60

E. Abbott Beede, Selectman:
Use of car, 146 miles at 5c	7.30
Dinner, Assessors' meeting	.40
Dinner, Portsmouth	.60

Eugene D. Sanborn, expenses as Trustee of
Trust Funds	5.00

$352.22

ELECTION AND REGISTRATION

Austin E. Carlton, ballot inspector	$3.00
Gladys B. Ahearn, ballot inspector	3.00
Sarah L. Clement, ballot inspector	3.00
Curtice S. Sanborn, supervisor	15.00
Sylvester A. Sanborn, supervisor	15.00
Arthur A. Davies, supervisor	15.00
Sargent Bros., printing ballots, 1936-1937.....	13.00
Edson C. Eastman Co., checklists	8.00
	$75.00

TOWN HALL

Regular Expenses:

N. H. Gas & Electric Co., lights	$63.72
Ralph S. True, 5 cords wood at $7.00......	35.00
E. Abbott Beede, 7 cords wood at $6.50	45.50
Arthur S. Moore, sawing and housing wood..	15.25
Lee B. Moulton, janitor	175.22
A. D. LeComte, fire insurance premium, 3 years	62.50
Frank H. Bray, painting flag pole	15.00
	$412.20

Toilet Installation:

Ernest W. Nye, plumbing and supplies	$148.99
W. E. Robertson, carpenter	22.50
Spaulding & Frost Co., supplies	28.87
H. J. Lawler Est., supplies	1.20
F. A. George Co., supplies	1.14
William T. Shannon, painting and supplies	6.70
George H. French, wiring and supplies ...	11.50
Virgil Davis, labor	18.10
Exeter Lumber Co., lumber, etc.	21.00
	$260.00
Total Town Hall expense........	$672.20

POLICE DEPARTMENT
Robert W. Smith, Chief

Use of car	$22.16
Duties	24.75
Telephone	2.40
	$49.31

FIRE DEPARTMENT
Robert W. Smith, Chief

EXPENSES:

Batteries charged, gas, oil, etc.	$15.71
Bell, in house and hall	4.20
Labor	43.60
Paid, Forest Smith	.75
Leslie Marcotte	1.55
Arthur Davies	13.80
F. Carrol Heselton	11.28
	$90.89
John T. J. Schon, watching fire	2.00
Warren E. Smith, Trailer	7.00
Spaulding & Frost Co., expenses of telephone	14.40
	$114.29

FIRE HOUSE

Appropriation 1937		$700.00
Spaulding & Frost Co., labor and supplies	$577.01	
Charles Kimball's Store, material	33.11	
Sylvester A. Sanborn, truck	5.00	
H. H. Gove, labor & cement mixer	26.00	
H. J. Lawler, Est., cement	13.05	
Exeter Lumber Co., cement	22.75	
		$676.92

FIRE HOSE

Appropriation	$300.00
Boston Woven Hose Rubber Co., 1000 ft.	
hose, less 2% $441.00	
Fremont Fire Department,	
Reimbursed town 141.00	$300.00

FOREST FIRE

Robert W. Smith, Warden

Posting Notice	$3.68

STREET LIGHTING

Paid N. H. Gas & Electric Co., service to date ..	$300.00

GENERAL EXPENSES OF HIGHWAY DEPARTMENT

Sylvester A. Sanborn, plowing snow, etc.	$76.74
Lyman S. Hooke, labor on snow plow	
and insurance	14.58
Blake's Place, gas for tractor	4 29
John B. Varick Co., supplies	14.09
Hume Pipe of New England Inc.	19.20
Merrimack Farmer's Exchange, shovels .	**10.50**
Alexander Supply Co., road machine	
blade	7.70
Southwestern Petroleum Co., Inc., oil ..	19.33
Nashua Steam Press & Boiler Works,	
repairing grousers	111.00
Dyar Sales & Machine Co., blade	9 90
Spaulding & Frost Co., supplies and	
labor	6.76
F. Carrol Heselton, labor & parts	18.38
Tractor Garage	$312.47

Ralph E. Kelly, labor & material 126.21
Sylvester A. Sanborn, labor & truck .. 40.40

$166.61

Total General Expenses of Dept. $479.08
　New Equipment:
　　Appropriation—for truck plow $270.00
　　Paid Austin Western Road
　　　Machine Co. $270.00

LIBRARY

Paid.

Lula M. Ball $50.00
N. H. Gas & Electric Co. .... --12.00
Ralph S. True, wood 7.00
H. J. Lawler Est., supplies 2.37
Exeter Lumber Co., lumber 9.54
Arthur S. True, for shelves 6.00

$86.91

CHARITIES

Appropriation $1,000.00

Town Poor.

Willard E. Porter, family
Mrs. Arthur E. Richards, Rent $96.00
John H. Ellis, groceries 416.00
J. P. Barrett, milk 60.88
H. J. Lawler Est., shoes & etc. 17.99
Ralph E. True, wood 14.00
Sylvester A. Sanborn, wood 3.75
J. P. Barrett, plowing, seed & etc. 24.98
John H. Ellis, seed 3.47

$637.07

John T. J. Schon, family
Sylvester A. Sanborn, wood $6.50
11. J. Lawler, Est., groceries 41.59

                                                      $48.09

Basil Keniston
Eli Marcotte, oil $1.80
H. J. Lawler, Est., groceries 21.31

                                                      $23.11

Arthur Billings
H. J. Lawler, Est., groceries $9.19

                                                      $9.19

Charles West,
F. A. George Co., groceries $45.78

Allen Moody,
Freeman B. Emerson, groceries 4.92

Edmund LaVoie,
F. A. George Co., groceries 40.02

Joseph Roche,
J. D. LeComte, milk $7.40
Arthur S. Moore, digging grave 3.00
Bertrand Peabody, burial of infant ..   30.00

                                                      $40.40

Edward J. Smith,
J. D. LeComte, milk $23.09
Chas. W. Hesleton, wood 16.00
Sylvester A. Sanborn, sawing wood ...   2.50
Ralph E. True, wood 14.00

                                                      $55.59
Albert G. Fuller, Administrator of Relief $35.00

H. J. Lawler, Est., feeding tramps 1.61
E. Albert Beede, returning grates 2.50
Albert G. Fuller, feeding tramps 2.95

$946.24
Reimbursed by State $184.49
Net Expense of town poor to town $761.75
Old Age Assistance paid by town $268.80

MEMORIAL DAY

Appropriation $160.00
Received for dinners 6.00
Contributions 19.22

$185.22

Expenditures:
Higgins band, H. F. Soule, leader 100.00
Speaker, Rev. Allen Lorimer 15.00
Rev. M. V. Granger 3.00
Freeman B. Emerson, Flags and
supplies 12.67
John B. Varick Co., flag...... 25.88
H. J. Lawler Est., supplies 16.12
F. A. George Co., supplies 3.49
John H. Ellis, supplies 4.06
Bertha L . True, labor 5.00

$185.22

CEMETERIES

Appropriation $65.00
Emedie Beaulieu, mowing
cemetery $6.00
Sylvester A. Sanborn, mowing &
cleaning yards 37.80

Arthur S. Moore, mowing &
    cleaning yards 29.00

                                  $72.80

UNCLASSIFIED

Refunds:

Jennie W. West, automobile tax $4.25

Abatements:

Helen Nichols, on property tax 7 50
Paid Laurence A. Pettengill, Collector,
    poll tax abatements 42.00

1937 *Poll Tax List*:

Grace E. Bishop, residence in Kingston 2.00
Perley C. Hamlin, residence in Ohio 2.00
Harriet F. Hamlin, residence in Ohio 2.00
Alice M. Brown, over seventy years of age ..   2.00
William Rankin, over seventy years of age ..   2.00
Carl G. Orfield, whereabouts unknown 2.00
Hazel Orfield, whereabouts unknown 2.00
Nettie M. Kimball, paid in Danville 2.00
Allen P. Moody, paid in Erving, Mass. 2.00
Alice G. Moody, residence in Mass. 2.00
Albert Pollard, paid in Raymond 2.00
Edward A. Towle, paid in Chester 2.00
Elbridge S. Young, paid in Farmington 2.00
Ruth M. Young, paid in Farmington 2.00

1936 *Poll Tax List*:

Alice E. Hayes, whereabouts unknown 2.00
John Collins, whereabouts unknown 2.00
Arthur C. Davis, whereabouts unknown 2.00
David Riddell, whereabouts unknown 2.00
Florida Riddell, whereabouts unknown 2.00
Elbridge S. Young, residence Brentwood ..   2.00
Ruth M. Young, residence Brentwood 2.00

STATE HIGHWAY CONSTRUCTION

Expenditures:

S. A. Sanborn, foreman	$226.75
S. A. Sanborn, truck	124.80
Clara B. Sanborn, truck	488.40
J. P. Bassett, truck	465.60
Arthur Billings, labor	166.00
Charles Healey, labor	111.20
Arthur S. Moore, labor	174.80
Basil Kenniston, labor	113.00
Emery W. Porter, labor	62.40
Henry Metavier, labor	102.60
Henry E. Smith, labor	56.00
Howard Tuttle, labor	150.60
E. Abbott Beede, labor	149.40
Alonzo B. Bishop, labor	110.40
William H. Rankin, labor	103.60
John T. J. Schon, labor	76.00
Horace St. John, truck	168.00
George F. Rogers, Jr., labor	117.80
Eugene E. West, labor	97.00
Lawrence E. West, labor	105.00
Lewis E. Robinson, labor	79.00
Edmund LaVoie, labor	67.40
Urban Metevier, labor	18.80
George W. Towle, labor	41.60
George W. Denyon, labor	21.60
George R. Copp, labor	25.60
Amedee C. Quintal, blacksmith work	6.50
W. L. Belanger, grading	12.60
Horace Goss, grading	46.80
Henry J. Lawler's Estate, cement, lime, oil, etc.	11.14
Lyman S. Hooke, sand for tar	2.00
Arthur S. Moore, sand for tar	2.50

S. A. Sanborn, dynamite, caps, etc. 6.28
Cora P. Falconer, gravel 26.50
Ernest S. Beede Estate, gravel 100.20
John H. Ellis, gravel 83.30
State Highway Garage, pipe 260.86
New England Metal Co., pipe 17.99
American Tar 442.37

$4,442.39

	State	Town	Total
Appropriations:	$3,000.00	$1,500.00	$4,500.00
Expended	2,951.99	1,490.40	4,442.39
Unexpended Balance ...	48.01	9.60	49.01

Taxes Bought by Town:

Gertrude F. Fellows, 6 lots of land $18.25
George N. Woodard Jr. 6.41
Winnefred E. Mills 6.41
Jacob G. Brown 5.65
Charles E. West 12.51
Leonard Rock 15.56
Allen P. Moody 15.56
John S. Keen Est. 21.66
Gertrude F. Langley 115.84

Taxes paid by Town:

Elizabeth C. Jackson 12.08
Sarah A. Guyette Est. 15.26

$245.19

REPORT OF FIRE CHIEF

In submitting my annual report as part of the permanent records, I wish to thank all who have helped on fires and on our fire house.

The fire truck was used six times; one grass fire at Clara Towle's, two chimney fires and two house fires.

I am sorry that the Mould house on the Chester road was

burned, but this was no fault of the fire department because the house was all burned before anyone saw the fire.

The Wilbur house at the North side would have burned the same way if no one had seen the fire.

I feel that it would be money well spent to send someone from the fire department around the town after every heavy thunder shower to look over the vacant houses.

REPORT OF FIRE WARDEN

I am glad to report that we did not have any brush fires during 1937.

Out of twenty eight permits issued, there were two fires which got out of control, but I am glad to say that from quick action on the part of the fire department they were quickly extinguished and no damage was done.

We had a good year, the best one since I have been Fire Warden. A hot dry summer is predicted so lets all try and keep this record during 1938.

Remember, "no person shall kindle or cause to be kindled any fire or shall burn or cause to be burned any material in or near any wood lands, pasture, brush, or where the fire may be communicated to such land except when the ground is covered with snow, without obtaining written permission from the Fire Warden. Whoever causes or kindles a fire by any means wilfully or in a careless and imprudent manner which shall endanger woodlands shall be fined not more than five hundred dollars or imprisoned not more than one year, or both."

Respectfully submitted,
ROBERT SMITH

HIGHWAY AGENT'S REPORT

SYLVESTER A. SANBORN, *Agent*

MAINTENANCE

S. A. Sanborn, truck	$581.32
S. A. Sanborn, labor	10.30
J. P. Bassett, truck	184.20
C. S. Sanborn, team	30.20
C. S. Sanborn, labor	69.00
Leonard Rock, labor	119.80
Basil Kenniston, labor	10.60
Henry E. Smith, labor	6.40
Lewis E. Robinson, labor	16.60
Edmund LaVoie, labor	23.40
John Campbell, labor	19.20
Charles Page, labor	19.80
Merton C. Healey, labor	3.00
Ralph W. Rogers, labor	.60
George F. Rogers, Jr., labor	33.40
Howard Tuttle, labor	18.60
Arthur Billings, labor	100.40
Alonzo B. Bishop, labor	103.80
Arthur Moore, labor	85.00
John T. J. Schon, labor	23.80
Henry Matavier, labor	120.80
Charles G. Healey, labor	103.60
Sidney Bishop, labor	2.00
George Denyou, labor	17.80
Charles E. West, labor	26.00
Frank M. Davis, labor and parts on road machine	2.45
S. A. Sanborn, express on road blade	2.32
Henry J. Lawler Est., cement	.80

Ernest S. Beede's Est., gravel 3.50
M. A. Willey, gravel 3.50
F. W. Falconer, gravel ....,... · 22.00
Lyman S. Hooke, gravel 1.50
J. H. Ellis, gravel ....~....... 16.00
Moses A. Seavey, gravel ....:.............. 12.50

$1,794.19

REPORT OF JANITOR OF TOWN HALL

I have .received for rental of the Town Hall for the year
as follows:

Two Community Club whist parties at $3.00...	$6.00
Six Grange whist parties at $2.50	15.00
Two Firemen's whist parties at $1.50	3.00
Three dances—Harold Beane and Victor Marcotte at $3.50	10.50
Seven dances—Harold Beane at $3.50........	24.50
Two dances—George C. Spalding at $3.50....	7.00
Twenty-six Grange meetings including one Pomona, one Juvenile at $2.50	65.00
Two extension service meetings at $1.50..:....	3.00
Six Jr. O. U. A. M. minstrel show rehearsals at $2.00	12.00
Two Jr. O. U. A. M. minstrel shows at $3.50..	7.00
Six Jr. O. U. A. M. meetings at $3.50	21.00
Two Grange rehearsals at $2.00.............	4.00
One Rockingham County Forest Fire Warden meeting and supper at $1.50 ....:....	1.50
One school play rehearsal at $2.00	2.00
One school play at $3.00	3.00
Three Townsend meetings, Charlie Heath at $3.50 ....:......................	10.50
One 4-H Club Leaders' meeting at $1.50	1.50
One Garden Club rehearsal at $2.00	2.00
One Garden Club entertainment at $3.50......	3.50

One Epworth League entertainment at $3.00	3.00
One penny supper, Community Club at $1.50	1.50
One lawn party, Church, at $1.00	1.00
One Beane reunion, Bertha Stevenson at $3.50	3.50
Six drama rehearsals, Grange, at $2.00........	12.00
Two Grange Fairs at $2.50	5.00
One Jacola Players at $5.00	5.00
One Farm Bureau and Community Club supper at $3.00	3.00
One harvest dinner and supper at $3.00.......	3.00
One Firemen's Ball at $1.50	1.50
Three drama rehearsals—Sunday School at $2.00	6.00
One drama, Sunday School at $3.00........	3.00
Seven drama rehearsals, Community Club at $2.00	14.00
Two dramas, Community Club at $3.00.......	6.00
One Sunday School Christmas Tree at $3.00..	3.00
One deputy sheriff's meeting at $1.50	1.50
	$274.00

The hall has been opened twenty times without charge for Selectmen, Supervisors, School Meeting, Town Meetings, Memorial Day and Schools.

Respectfully submitted,

LEE B. MOULTON, *Janitor*

Report of the Trust Funds of the Town of Fremont, N. H., on January 31, 1938

Date of Creation	TRUST FUNDS—Name PURPOSE of FUND	HOW INVESTED	Amount of Principal	Rate of Interest	Balance of Income on Hand at Beginning of Year	Income During Year	Expended During Year	Balance of Income on Hand at End of Year
1873 Aug. 28	The Sarah A. Chase, "Universalist Fund"	okeag Savings Bank ster Savings Bank	$500.00 500.00	3% "	$7.54 7.54	$ 1511 15.11	$15.15 15.15	$7.50 7.50
Aug. 23	The Sarah A. Chase, "Worthy Poor Fund"	ag Savings Bank Manchester Sngs Bank	700.00 606.01	" "	102.79 80.55	22.86 22.78	94.47 49.23	31.18 54.10
1915 Dec. 15	The Mary R. Chase "Cemetery Fund"	moskeag Savings Bank	100.00	"	3.04	3.11	.....	6.15
1917 May 31	The Josiah B. Robinson "Methodist Fund"	Amoskeag Savings Bank Man ster Savings Bank	1,300.00 1,200.00	" "	19.60 18.09	39.29 36.27	39.39 36.36	190 8.00
May 31	The Aaron J. Robinson "Cemetery Fund"	ag Savings Bank New Hampshire Savings Bank Merrimack River Savings Bank	2,000.00 688.55 370.74	" "	..... 11.90	60.45 21.02	60.45 16.60	16.32 .....
1920 May 1	The Mary Susan Higgins "Modist Fund"	Am g Savings Bank	2,000.00	"	30.15	60.45	60.60	30.00
Nov. 3	The My Susan Higgins "Cemetery Fund"	ag Savings Bank	100.00	"	30.62	3.92	4.53	30.01
1923 Aug. 22	1 ... A. Scribner "Cemetery Fund"	eag Savings Bank	300.00	"	110.69	12.36	10.89	112.16

1926							
Sept. 9	The George W. Robie "Cemetery Fund"	Amoskeag Savings Bank ...	200.00	"	41.36	7.27	5.52	43.11
1928 April 1	The James W. Burleigh "Cemetery Fund"	Mechanics Savings Bank ...	100.00	"	6.44	3.21	....	9.65
Oct. 1	The Frank D. Rowe "Cemetery Fund"	Mechanics Savings Bank ..	250.00		29.81	8.50	7.46	30.85
1933 Nov. 24	The Horace G. & Arthur R. Whittier "Cemetery Fund"	Manchester Savings Bank ..	200.00		12.90	6.42	3.50	15.82
1935 Sept. 23	The Wilcomb H. Benfield "Cemetery Fund", ...	Manchester Savings Bank ..	100.00		.32	3.02	3.14	.20
Nov. 26	The Jonathan A. Robinson "Cemetery Fund"	Manchester Savings Bank ...	100.00	"	.66	3.03	2.38	1.31

DETAILED STATEMENT OF PAYMENTS
OF TRUST FUNDS

The Sarah A. Chase "Universalist Fund:

Henry A. Cook, Treasurer University Society $30.30

The Sarah A. Chase "Worthy Poor Fund":

F. A. George Co., groceries G. W. Amerige and
mother 6.00
Fremont Dairy, milk, Edmond Lavoie........   8.40
H. J. Lawler Est., groceries, Edmond Lavoie..   55.72
H. J. Lawler Est., groceries, Arthur Billings
and family 49.23
Fremont Dairy, milk, Edmond Lavoie 14.40
F. A. George & Co., groceries, Charles West..   9.95

The Josiah B. Robinson "Methodist Fund":

Nellie P. Bassett, Treasurer People's M. E.
Church 75.75

The Aaron J. Robinson "Cemetery Fund":

H. J. Lawler Est., fertilizer 8.75
Bartlett Greenhouse, plants and flowers......   7.50
Melvin P. Leavitt, labor (Leavitt yard)......   46.80
Melvin P. Leavitt, labor (Sleeper yard)......   14.00

The Mary Susan Higgins "Methodist Fund":

Nellie P. Bassett, Treasurer People's M. E.
Church 60.60

The Mary Susan Higgins "Cemetery Fund":

Carroll B. West, labor	1.13
Allen Copp, labor	.20
Charles G. Healey, labor	.50
E. D. Sanborn, labor	2.70

The Elizabeth A. Scribner "Cemetery Fund":

C. S. Sanborn, labor	1.38
Carroll B. West, labor	1.28
James Porter, labor	.40
Allen Copp, labor	1.11
E. D. Sanborn, labor	4.22
W. E. Coffin, fertilizer	2.50

The George W. Robie "Cemetery Fund":

E. D. Sanborn, labor	3.46
Charles G. Healey, labor	.65
Allen Copp, labor	.12
Carroll B. West, labor	1.29

The Frank D. Rowe "Cemetery Fund":

E. D. Sanborn, labor	3.05
Emery Porter, labor	1.00
Charles G. Healey, labor	.50
Allen Copp, labor	.96
Carroll B. West, labor	1.66
C. S. Sanborn, labor	.29

The Horace G. & Arthur R. Whittier "Cemetery Fund":

William J. Philbrick, labor	2.50
E. D. Sanborn, labor	1.00

The Wilcomb H. Benfield "Cemetery Fund":

Carroll B. West, labor	1.40
Allen Copp, labor	.26
E. D. Sanborn, labor	1.48

The Jonathan A. Robinson "Cemetery Fund":

C. S. Sanborn, labor	.29
Carroll B. West, labor	.62
Russell Copp, labor	.12
E. D. Sanborn, labor	1.35

EUGENE D. SANBORN,
HENRY A. COOK,
ALBERT G. FULLER,
Trustees of Trust Funds.

REPORT OF AUDITOR

I have examined the books and accounts of the Selectmen, Treasurer, Town Clerk, Tax Collector, Highway Agent, Forest Wire Warden, Janitor of the Town Hall and the Trustees of Trust Funds of the Town of Fremont for the fiscal year ending January 31st, 1938, and find them correctly cast and supported by proper vouchers. All funds and evidences of funds were tabulated and found as represented.

Fremont, N. H., February 10th., 1938.

NORMAN S. McINTOSH,
Auditor

REPORT OF LIBRARIAN

Total number of books in library	3,070
Total number of cards issued	280
Issued during year	13
Circulation	3,011
Cash on hand Feb. 1, 1937	.29

Received for fines during year $4.44
Received from Library Trustees 40.00

$44.73

Paid out for books $40.00
Incidental expenses 4.58

$44.58

Cash on hand Feb. 1, 1938 .... $.15

B. MAY MARCOTTE,
Librarian.

REPORT OF LIBRARY TRUSTEES

Received from the Selectmen................ $50.00
Paid Librarian for books $40.00
For magazine subscriptions 10.00

$50.00

LULA M. BELL,
Treasurer.

Annual Reports

OF THE

Officers

OF THE

Fremont School District

For the Year
July 1, 1936 to June 30,1937

OFFICERS OF FREMONT SCHOOL DISTRICT

1937-1938

School Board
NORMAN S. McINTOSH, Chr., Term expires 1938
MRS. DOROTHY SANBORN, Term expires 1939
MRS. HELEN SEAVEY, Term expires 1940

Superintendent of Schools
HAROLD C. BOWLEY

Treasurer
GEORGE BEEDE

Moderator
E UGENE D. SANBORN

Clerk
BERTHA L. TRUE

Auditor
FLORENCE A. GEORGE

Attendance Officer
ROBERT SMITH

Enumerator
DOROTHY T. SANBORN

School Nurse
CONSTANCE COOPER, R. N.

39

SCHOOL WARRANT

THE STATE OF NEW HAMPSHIRE

To the Inhabitants of the School District in the Town of Fremont qualified to vote in district affairs:

You are hereby notified to meet at the Fremont Town Hall, in said district, on the 7th day of March, 1938, at 7:30 o'clock in the afternoon, to act upon the following subjects:

1. To choose a Moderator for the coming year.
2. To choose a Clerk for the ensuing year.
3. To choose a Member of the School Board for the ensing three years.
4. To choose a Treasurer for the ensuing year.
5. To determine and appoint the salaries of the School Board and truant officer, and fix the compensation of any other officers or agent of the district.
6. To hear the reports of Agents, Auditors, Committees, or officers chosen, and pass any vote relating thereto.
7. To choose Agents, Auditors and Committees in relation to any subject embraced in this warrant.
8. To see if the district will vote to make any alteration in the amount of money required to be assessed for the ensuing year for the support of public schools and the payment of the statutory obligations of the district, as determined by the School Board in its annual report.

To transact any other business which may legally come before this meeting.

Given under our hands at said Fremont this 27th day of January, 1938.

NORMAN S. McINTOSH,
DOROTHY T. SANBORN,
HELEN SEAVEY,

School Board

SCHOOL BOARD BUDGET

From July 1, 1938 to June 30, 1939

To be voted on at annual school meeting March 7, 1938 at 7:30 P. M.

Teachers' salaries	$3,671.00
Textbooks	150.00
Scholars' supplies	150.00
Flags and appurtenances	5.00
Other expenses of instruction	20.00
Janitor service	144.00
Fuel	150.00
Water, light, janitors' supplies	90.00
Minor repairs and expenses	100.00
Health supervision	190.00
Transportation of pupils	800.00
Other special activities	20.00

Total for "support of schools"		$5,490.00
Deduct State Aid	$1,625.00	
Deduct dog licenses	175.00	
		$1,800.00

Balance to raise by district tax for support of schools	$3,690.00
Salaries of district officers	115.00
Superintendent's excess salary	200.00
Truant officer, school census	25.00
Expenses of administration	35.00
High school tuitions	3,055.00
Per capita tax	232.00
	$7,352.00

Reduction proposed by School Board 1,352.00

Grand total to raise by district tax for all
    school purposes $6,000.00

Respectfully submitted,

NORMAN S. McINTOSH,
DOROTHY T. SANBORN,
HELEN P. SEAVEY,
School Board

January 27, 1938

SCHOOL BOARD'S FINANCIAL STATEMENT

July 1, 1936 to June 30, 1937

RECEIPTS

Cash on hand July 1, 1936	$1,318.67
Equalization Fund	1,616.01
District tax for:	
Support of elementary schools	497.00
Payment of high school tuitions	1,800.00
Salaries of district officers	115.00
Payment of interest on debt	228.00
$2 per capita tax	360.00
Balance of previous appropriations	2,000.00
Dog licenses	180.00
Total receipts	$8,114.68

PAYMENTS

Salaries of district officers	$115.00
Superintendent's excess salary	200.00
Truant officers and school census	25.00
Expenses of administration	30.94

Principals' and teachers' salaries	3,675.26
Text Books	149.48
Scholars' supplies	151.19
Flags and appurtenances	3.00
Other expenses of instruction	11.02
Janitor service	144.00
Fuel	142.06
Water, light, janitor's supplies	87.87
Minor repairs and expenses	147.11
Medical inspection	201.79
Transportation of pupils	656.60
High School and Academy tuitions	1,757.77
Other special activities	30.84
$2 per capita tax	228.00
Alterations of old buildings ....,....	106.00
Cash on hand at end of year June 30, 1937....	251.75
Total payments	$8,114.68

HAROLD C. BOWLEY,
Superintendent

NORMAN S. McINTOSH,
DOROTHY T. SANBORN,
HELEN SEAVEY,
School Board

AUDITOR'S CERTIFICATE

This is to certify that I have examined the books and other financial records of the School Board of Fremont, of which this is a true summary for the fiscal year ending June 30, 1937, and find them correctly cast and properly vouched.

FLORENCE A. GEORGE,
Auditor

July 14, 1937

REPORT OF DISTRICT TREASURER

For the Year Ending June 30, 1937

Cash on hand June 30, 1936	$1,318.67
Received from:	
Selectmen, appropriations for current year	3,000.00
Balance of previous appropriation	2,000.00
Dog tax	180.00
State Treasurer	1,616.01
Total amount available for fiscal year....	$8,114.68
Less School Board orders paid	7,862.93
Balance on hand as of June 30, 1937....	$251.75
Balance due from town	2,102.00
Total assets	$2,353.75

GEORGE E. BEEDE,
Treasurer

July 13, 1937

AUDITOR'S CERTIFICATE

This is to certify that I have examined the books, vouchers, bank statements and other financial records of the treasurer of the school district of Fremont of which the above is a true summary for the fiscal year ending June 30, 1937 and find them correct in all respects.

FLORENCE A. GEORGE,
Auditor

July 14, 1937

REPORT OF SUPERINTENDENT

To the School Board and Citizens of Fremont:

I herewith present my eleventh annual report as Superintendent of Schools.

INSTRUCTION

At this time last year, we were working with a substitute teacher for Mrs. Towle, due to the latter's serious accident. Indeed fortunate was the district to have available for substitute duty one with experience and adaptability of Mrs. Edna K. French, of Sandown. Mrs. French completed the school year for Mrs. Towle. This year a like situation prevails. Miss Helen Noyes of Plaistow, a 1937 graduate of Keene Normal School, was employed to take the place of Miss Stevenson at the Primary School. Miss Noyes suffered an attack of pneumonia in December and is as yet unable to return to her duties, with Mrs. French again acting as substitute. Miss Noyes came to us with the best of qualifications and recommendations. This promise of development into an excellent teacher appeared to be justified when this illness came upon her. It is to be regretted that she has been detained so long from the duties she loved so well. I am sure I bespeak your wishes that she may be speedily returned to normal health and strength.

Miss Stevenson leaves the profession after an honorable period of ten years as a teacher for you and two other communities. She has performed her work well and deserves the commendation of her colleagues and employers. We wish her well in her new activities.

The remainder of the teaching force is the same as last year without change.

This topic of Instruction brings to mind the activities and progress of the children in school. As a whole, 89% received promotion, in June 1937, 7% trial promotion, and 4% non-promotion. A study of the reading abilities and capacities of grades 2-7 inclusive, was conducted. .

In this important tool subject, it was found that 4 percent of these children were far below grade, and some 14 percent more were experiencing some difficulty in one form or other. In the main the former group show very little comprehension while the latter have trouble to fully appreciate the material read. Certain tests were given and the correlation of results is close between the tests given in schools through the year with these special tests. This gives additional evidence that the reports rendered to parents every six weeks have not been in error to any great extent. We must aim at and strive to achieve a literate America. So, this furthers our intent to make our pupils read and fires our ambitions to contribute toward this objective. I do not wish to convey that these pupils do not read at all, but rather that they do not read as well as they should in their grade. The results are not as unfavorable as the Union, as a whole, yet are important enough to demand attention and a desire for improvement. Examination of the scores leads us to a belief that some children enter school before the proper mental age. It is recognized that a child must be six years old mentally to accomplish the work of the first grade, and then progress step by step through the remaining grades. Some children reach this readiness age at 5, others at 6 and still others at 7 or later years. This school program is built with an understanding of this readiness period from the first grade through the university. Therefore, it is possible, an adjustment is in order either to fit the program to the pupils as they are admitted or to determine some definite scheme to show their readiness before they begin. The former is expensive in that failures and lowering of standards result; the latter difficult to administer in that some pupils are not admitted until a year or more later than their playmates. Just which procedure is the safer is now a matter of conjecture and controversy. There may be a solution of the problem as time goes on.

Perfect Attendance

I am pleased to list the following pupils as perfect in attendance during 1936-37 and to include the parents' names as well:

Pupils	Parent
Carroll Hall	Allen Hall
Sherburne Gove	Howard Gove
Grace Pinet	Laura Pinet
Marion Beane	Harold Beane
Florence Clark	Leslie Clark
Eleanor Gove	Howard Gove
Walter Moulton	Lee Moulton
Beverly Smith	Roy Smith
Norman Healey	Merton Healey
Barbara Healey	Merton Healey
Marilyn Kreger	Mrs. Rilla Kreger
Clyde Bishop	Mrs. Fred Bishop

Information About 1936-37

Average percent of attendance	95.53
No. pupils enrolled	115
Average membership	99.04
No. of graduates	9
No. of graduates entering High school	8
Other pupils in high school	17
Visits by School Board	7
Visits by Superintendent	84
Visits by School Nurse	193
Visits by Music Teacher	66
Visits by others	146

Financial Data

I list for your information certain facts collected from State Board of Education and State Tax Commission reports as well as local reports. These show the financial burden to support schools and how well it is being done in comparison with other towns of this Union.

EQUALIZED VALUATION
Per Pupil 1937

New Hampshire	$8,842
East Kingston	6,041
South Hampton	5,839
Fremont	5,837
Kingston	5,307
Danville	4,731
Brentwood	4,613
Sandown	4,326
Epping	3,543

1937 Tax Rates

Epping	$4.45
Sandown	4.30
Kingston	4.30
Danville	3.70
East Kingston	3.46
N. H. Average	3.43
Brentwood	3.40
South Hampton	2.70
Fremont	2.60

PERCENT SCHOOL SUPPORT IS OF TOTAL TAX

South Hampton	43
Danville	40
Brentwood	36
Fremont	34
East Kingston	31
Epping	31
Kingston	29
Sandown	29
N. H. Average	26.6

PER PUPIL COSTS OF ELEMENTARY SCHOOLS 1936-37

South Hampton	100.08
East Kingston	84.53
Danville	81.18
Sandown	80.96
N. H. Median	77.16
Kingston	71.56
Fremont	60.60
Brentwood	60.45
Epping	49.60

ALL SCHOOL COSTS PER $1,000

	Equalized Valuation		
	Total	State Aid	Net
Danville	$19.55	$4.72	$14.83
Sandown	16.72	6.48	10.24
South Hampton	16.52	4.84	11.68
Epping	15.89	4.81	11.08
Danville	14.14	4.23	9.91
Eaast Kingston	13.88	3.44	10.44
Kingston	13.84	2.93	10.91
New Hampshire Median	11.74	.57	11.14
Fremont	11.25	2.50	8.76

CONCLUSIONS

I commend the School Board for its attitude toward the proper upkeep of the school buildings. A rather regular plan of painting and repair has been followed with the result that the rooms present a better appearance at all times and no major item of expense for repair comes all in one tax year.

In closing, I express my appreciation to the teachers for their very conscientious efforts during the past year and to the School Board for their active interest in the work of the schools and to my suggestions for improvement.

Please read the Health Report which follows.

Very respectfully,

HAROLD C. BOWLEY,

January 31, 1938

Supt. of Schools

HEALTH SUPERVISION

Of the 100 pupils eamined during the school year 1936-37, the following cases were found and treatments made:

	No. of Cases	No. of treatments or defects corrected
Underweight	8	8
Defective vision	9	9
Nervous condition	1	1
Defective teeth	31	31
Diseased tonsils	8	8
Defective breathing	2	2
Adenoids	8	8
Enlarged glands	11	10
Defective speech	1	
Measles	1	
Pediculosis	14	
Skin diseases	21	
Small Pox vaccinations	100	
Diphtheria toxin-antitoxin	89	

The dental clinic was financed by the Community Dental Committee.

No. pupils examined by dentist	65		
No. pupils needing extractions (temporary teeth)	13	(permanent)	3
No. pupils with cavities (temporary teeth)	11	(permanent)	29
No. pupils needing teeth cleaned	61		
Total number extractions (temporary teeth)	37	(permanent)	3
Total number cement fillings	20		
Total number amalgam fillings	71		
Total number porcelain fillings	4		

CONSTANCE COOPER, R. N.

Vital Statistics

BIRTHS REGISTERED IN THE TOWN OF FREMONT, N. H., FOR THE YEAR ENDING DECEMBER 31, 1937

Date of Birth 1937	Place of Birth	Name of the Child	Male or Fe.	Liv. or Stb.	No. of Child	Color	Name of Father	Maiden Name of Mother	Residence of Parents	Occupation of Father	Birthplace of Father	B...
6	Exeter	Janice Stevenson	F	L	1	W	Carl H. Stevenson	Mary Helfer	Fremont	Cooperage	Fremont	Ex
5	Exeter	Jacquelyn Moulton	F	L	4	W	Lee Brown Moulton	Florence Spaulding	Fremont	Stave Sawyer	Colorado	Fr
3	Exeter	Clifford Allen Copp	M	L	1	W	Allen Copp	Harriet Hays	Fremont	Laborer	Brentwood	Ro
14	Exeter	Carroll Russell West	M	L	1	W	Carroll West	Cora Copp	Fremont	Mill Worker	Fremont	Br
20	Exeter	Carolyn Ruth Kelley	F	L	2	W	Richard E. Kelley	Ruth Collins	Fremont	Barrel Fac. Em.	Fremont	E.
7	Exeter	Marie Alice Le Clair	F	L	1	W	James J. Le Clair	Alice Butrick	Fremont	Pail Maker	Fremont	N.
17	Exeter	Emily Frances Plante	F	L	2	W	Emil J. Plante	Frances O. Bailey	Fremont	Mill Employee	Wisconsin	Ex

I hereby certify that the above return is correct, according to the best of my knowledge and belief

WILLIAM T. SHANNON, T

Date	Place	Name and Surname of Groom and Bride	Place at time of Marriage	Age	Color	Occupation of Groom and Bride	Place of Birth of Each	Names of Parents	Birthplace of Parents	Occupation	By whom married
20	Hampstead	Ernest E. ...	Fremont	27	W	... age	Fremont	George J. LeClair	Ashburnham	...	Samuel ...
		Jessie May Rand	Fremont	26	W	Housework	Sandown	Albertha Sargent	Sandown	Housewife	1
10	Fremont	...ld A. Trafton	E. ...ad	2	W	...bier	Rochester	Frank E. Rand	Chester	Not living	2
3	Fremont	...lin ...ss	Haverhill, M.	20	W	At the	Haverhill, Ms.	Susan Sanborn / Ashton Trafton	Chester / Rochester	Br. / ...	W. T. Mini...
y	Fremont	Arthur ...n	...ondonderry	24	W	Farm ...hd	Roxbury, Ms.	Bertha Lord	Rochester	Shoeworker	Em... Frem...
		...le Mabry	Litchfield	18	W	At the	Nashua	Stanly Carter / ...e Berger	Haverhill / Haverhill	...	2
ly	Fremont	...d W. ...le	...ha	26	W	She	Nashua	...l ...n / ...ia Larsen	Norway / Norway	Rigger	W. T. Mi...
		...d ...nt	Tremont	19	W	At ...me	Fremont	Rexford Mabry / Hazel Smith	Maine / Concord	Not living	1 Elm...
ly	Fremont	Charles ...t	Boston, Ms.	23	W	Film worker	Boston, Mass.	Arthur W. Little / Ethel Martin	Hudson / Fremont	R. R. / Mill operator	1 Min... Frem...
		...a Carlson	W. Medford, Mass.	22	W	Film Insp'ct'r	W. Med., Ms.	Emma Jae Dorr	Derry	...	W. T. ...
ly	Tremont	Ralph Sargent	Plaistow	22	W	Tannery W'k'r	Plaistow	Annie Duran / Frank Carlson	South America / Ireland	Ho'el worker / Theatre	1 Em... Frem...
		...a ...n	W. Medford	21	W	At the	W. Med. Ms.	Lena ...r	Boston, Mass.	Fireman	W. T. Mi...
ly 24	Fremont	Norman A. ...e	W. Kingston	28	W	Cook	Everett, Mass.	...e Sargent / Susan Kent	Boston, Mass. / Sandown	Housewife / Not living	1 Elm... Frem...
		...s E. Braley	Tremont	23	W	Burler	Plaistow	Walter Newton / William F. Cline	Rowley, Mass. / Arlington, Ms.	Housewife / U. S. Navy	W. T. Mi...
ly 31	Tremont	...ie M. Rogers	...d	20	W	She worker	Raymond	Ethel ...t / Ella ...ttler	Somerville / Somerville	Not ...ing / Ice man	1 Elm... Frem...
		Barbara R. Hartford	...ng	...d	W	At the	Epping	...lph W. Rogers / Cora M. ...y	Not known / No. Andover	Housewife	W. T. Mi...
								...nd O. Hartford / ...e Foss	Epping / Epping / Epping	Nvy Yard / She worker	1 Elm...

Name	Residence		Age	C	Occupation	Other party	Residence	Birthplace	Occupation	Officiant	No.
Howard G. Tuttle	Fremont		50	W	Laborer	Walter H. Tuttle	Fremont	W. Epping	Not living	W. T. Shannon, Minister, Elm Terrace, Fremont N. H.	2
Clara L. West	Fremont		43	W	At home	Jennie M.	Lawr'nce, Ms.	Raymond	Not living	Elm Terrace, Fremont N. H.	2
James Miller, Jr.	Haverhill, Mass.		26	W	Manufacturer	George A. Whittier	Haverhill, Ms.	Newton	Not living	W. T. Shannon, Elm Terrace, Fremont N. H.	1
Ellen Lake	Haverhill, Mass.		22	W	Nurse	Ellen C. Paslee	E. H'm'n, Ms.	Kingston	Shoe pat. wkr.	Justice of the Peace, Fremont N. H.	1
William V. Snodgrass	Mass.		29	W	Accountant	James Fisher	Woon's't, R. I.	Scotland	Not living	S. B. Enman, W. Hampstead, Minister	1
Edith F. Stevenson	Fremont		29	W	Teacher	Johan Fisher		E. Hampton	Housewife	W. Hampstead, Minister	1
Robert B.	Fremont		23	W	office work	Ada Safran	Fremont	E. Hampton	Foreman		1
Dorothy L. Janvrin	Seabrook		23	W	At home	Harry Snodgrass	Fremont	Nova Scotia	Housewife	S. B. Enman, Hampstead, Minister	1
Nils Hokanson	Watertown, Mass.		30	W	Baker	Helen M. Mahoney		Fremont	Cooper		1
Carlson	Brighton, Mass.		30	W	Clerk	Lester G. Stevenson		E. Somerville	Housewife	W. T. Shannon, Elm Terrace, Fremont, N. H., Minister	1
Collins	Chelsea, Mass.		21	W	Seaman	Florence Mitchener		Chester	Not living	W. T. Shannon, Elm Terrace, Fremont, N. H.	1
Leaneita Seavey	Chelsea, Mass.		19	W	At home	Harry S.	Mass.	Fremont	Housewife	Justice of the Peace	1
James Papavacil	Haverhill, Mass.		21	W	Truck driver	Lena E. C.	Seabrook	Seabrook	Merchant	W. T. Shannon, Elm Terrace, Fremont, N. H.	1
Anna Mary Serratore	Haverhill, Mass.		23	W	At home	T Neal Janvrin	Seabrook	Sweden	Housewife	Justice of the Peace, Fremont, N. H.	1
Rutledge G. Frost	Fremont		33	W	Gas Sta. Prop	Helen	Sweden	Sweden	Fisherman	Samuel B. Enman, Hampstead, N. H.	2
Mid Elizabeth Plant	Raymond		20	W	Telegraph Op.	Nils Hokanson		Sweden	Housewife	Minister	1
John J. Dupre	Haverhill, Mass.		21	W	Shoe worker	Andrew F. Carlson	Cam'ge, Ms.	Sweden	Retired	W. T. Shannon, Elm Terrace, Fremont, N. H.	1
Julia P. Forgione	Haverhill, Mass.		21	W	At home	Catharine Dillon	Chelsea, Mass.	England	Steamfitter	Minister	1

rtify that the above return is correct, according to the best of my knowledge and belief.

WILLIAM T. SHANNON, *Town Clerk*

ive October 1, 1938, marriage intention must conform to laws of 1937 Chap. 36. All persons filing marriage intentions must doctor's certificate verifying the fact that they submitted to the Wasserman or Kahn laboratory blood test.

DEATHS REGISTERED IN THE TOWN OF FREMONT N. H., FOR THE YEAR ENDING DECEMBER 31, 1937

Date of Death	Place of Death	Name and Surname of the Deceased	Years	Months	Days	Place of Birth	Male or Fe.	Color	Sin. Mar. or Wid.	Occupation	Place of Birth of Father	Place of Birth of Mother	Name of Father	Maid
Feb. 8	Derry	Mha Rock	71	4	16	Fremont, N.H.	F	W	S		Kingston,	Brentwood	Joseph Rock	Emma
Mar. 28	Fremont	Henry W. Stevens	75	7	8	Raym'nd, N.H.	M	W	W	Carpenter	Raymond,	Exeter	John F.	Eliza
April 2	Fremont	Emma M. Cook	75	10	17	Brookline, N.H.	F	W	M	Housewife	Lun'b'g, Mass.	N. Y. City		Mls
July 26	Hampstead	Isabel C. Kimball	75	7	1		F							
Dec. 5	Fremont	Grl W. Beede	42	5	18	Fremont, N.H.	M	W	S	Laborer	Canada	Ch ster	Earnest S. Beede	Ali oe S
Dec. 21	Fremont	Doldry Robert Smith	82	1	4	Hadley Eng.	M	W	M	Laborer	England	England	Samuel	Sharlotte

I hereby certify that the above return is correct, aording to the best of my knowledge and belief.

WILLIAM T. SHANNON, *To*